Canetti Perfetti

Book 1:
Meet The Family

Canetti Perfetti: Book 1: Meet The Family

Copyright © 2024 by Debbie Levitt. All Rights Reserved.

No part of this book may be reproduced in any form or by any electronic or mechanical means including information storage and retrieval systems, without permission in writing from the author.

Book design by Piermario Orecchioni aka "Daddy"

Thanks to Terina Le Roux, Leah Eva and her mom Lali, Mia, Kelene, Lisa, and Isla for early book feedback.

This book is non-fiction, based on our real world and our real dogs. No photos were staged.
No AI was used to generate, enhance, or alter any text or photos.

Visit us at CanettiPerfetti.com or
@CanettiPerfetti on Instagram.

Paperback ISBN 978-1-7340977-7-1

This book is dedicated to
and in memory of
my mother, Linda Naponelli.

A warm heart, and
the best dog auntie to
every pup she met.

I'm Olivia.

My family adopted me when I was just a few months old.

They also adopted my brother, **Romeo**.

I want to tell you all about my family.

Romeo and I live in the countryside with our human Mommy and Daddy.

It's a relaxing and quiet place with trees, hills, and farms.

We are in Italy.
Is Italy far away from where you live?

When I was older, I had seven beautiful puppies.

Some looked quite different from each other.

Puppies that have the same Mom sometimes have different Dads, but they are still brothers and sisters.

At two weeks old, six boys and one girl were given names.

What names would you give them?

ORSO POLARE
(OR-so po-LAH-reh)

This puppy was all white so he was named Orso Polare. That means "polar bear" in Italian.

JUNIOR
(JOO-nyor)

This boy was called Junior because he looked like a mini-Olivia.

PISOLO
(PEE-zoh-loh)

In Italian, Pisolo is "Sleepy" from "Snow White and the Seven Dwarfs."

There was a set of twins.

GALILEO (gah-lih-LEH-oh)

Galileo was the first puppy to open his eyes. He was named after a scientist who lived hundreds of years ago.

CAFFELATTE (cah-feh-LAH-teh)

Caffelatte means "coffee with milk" in Italian. That matched his colors.

Diana was the only girl. Even at two weeks old, she played just as roughly as the boys.

DIANA (dee-AH-nah)

She never felt afraid. Diana was the first to try new things.

Teseo was always a thoughtful pup that considered others first. He was very polite and liked to wait his turn.

TESEO (teh-ZAY-oh)

He had a big imagination.

Nine dogs are just too many! So we gave some puppies away to nice families.

(cah-NET-tee per-FEHT-tee)

Romeo

Pisolo, Diana, and Teseo stayed with us.

We call our dog family, "Canetti Perfetti," which is one way to say "perfect puppies" in Italian.

And they are!

We have a big, fenced area outside. There are three dog houses. Diana usually shares a house with her brother, Pisolo.

It's me, Olivia! I decided that I don't want to live inside the fence.

I learned to climb fences so I could leave!

During the day, I run around and visit neighbors and dog friends.

Sometimes I explore so far away that I end up near the lake! I don't like to swim, so I turn around and head back.

Let's meet the family!

I'm Diana. I am small, but I am the smartest. Everybody follows me.

I plan our escapes. No fence can hold me for long! I have friends to go see!

You already know me. I'm Olivia! I have my own fort made out of a small table and some blankets.

It's my special hiding and sleeping place.

Look at me! I'm Pisolo. I like to run fast and crash into things.

I follow what everybody else is doing, but I'll find a way to stand out.

I'm Romeo. I'm Olivia's brother, and the uncle of Teseo, Diana, and Pisolo.

I am a watchdog. I don't keep secrets. I have different barks that announce what's going on... like escapes!

I supervise all of the work and repairs. Diana makes a lot of escape holes in the fences. Daddy needs my help when he's fixing things.

Some people have trouble telling the dogs apart. Do you know their names?

I like to run around during the day, and sleep at home.

I like to watch people work, and announce Diana's escapes.

"I like to chew holes in fences. I always have a smart plan."

"I am very silly, and I like to copy what others are doing."

"I like to imagine big adventures. I'm also relaxed and patient."

Meet Our Friends!

We have made a lot of dog friends where we live. We love to visit them when we escape our yard.

Like Olivia, some dogs live in houses. Some live outside like the rest of the Canetti Perfetti family.

But some dogs have jobs!
They have important things to do on farms and ranches.

STELLA (STEHL-lah)

I'm Stella and I'm only one year old.

I look serious, but I love to jump and bite. I don't bite hard. I'm only playing.

I'm Vasco. I'm always happy to see Olivia on my street!

Today, I have a piece of pizza. Do not steal it from me! I'm watching you!

VASCO (VAHS-coh)

Olivia's Daddy gave me a nice face rub.

Oh no! There is a cow! Stay away, cow.

Maybe the cow is jealous of the attention I'm getting.

BITTER
(BEE-tehr)

I'm Bitter! Well, that's the name I was given.

Sometimes I am grumpy.

Once, seven puppy brothers and sisters showed up at our house. They had escaped, and were thirsty.

Their Daddy came in his truck to bring everybody home.

I'm Joker, and I'm sure I'm Olivia's best friend.

I live across the street.

They once followed us home.
The Canetti Perfetti family was very surprised to see them.

All of the Canetti Perfetti dogs are kind to Lulù.

She is part of the family.

Sometimes the donkeys from up the street come to see if we have any snacks for them.

They are very friendly, and love to eat vegetables.

How to Steal Pancakes

By Diana

First, jump up on the chair all by yourself, and sit nicely at the table.

Pretend you don't notice that Daddy is eating delicious, homemade blueberry pancakes.

I was not sneaky enough!
Daddy figured out what I'm trying to do.
"Diana, no no no!"

He gave me a nice boop on my nose with his finger.

Maybe I can still get those pancakes.

Other Silly Adventures

Once I was stuck in the neighbor's yard behind some thorny sticks.

Mommy had to lift me up to help me get out.

Being out in the country helps us have plenty of space. We love being active and outdoors.

We love our home, and our Mommy and Daddy.

But we love escaping too!

Canetti Perfetti are perfect puppies.
A silly, cuddly, and sweet family.
Sometimes we get in trouble.
But every day is a fun
and wild adventure
in a little Italian village.

Draw your favorite dog!

Draw a beautiful place with a lake.

Draw something funny a dog dreams of doing.

www.ingramcontent.com/pod-product-compliance
Lightning Source LLC
Chambersburg PA
CBHW080325080526
44585CB00021B/2472